SHOW RIDER

SHOW RIDER

words by

LYNN HANEY

photographs by

BRUCE CURTIS

G. P. Putnam's Sons, New York

ACKNOWLEDGMENTS

For their generous and skillful contributions to the preparation
of this book we would like to thank the following: Bill and Elissa Cibbarelli,
John and Merilee Ventura, John Trowbridge, Judge Penny Rosenthal
and Steward Jim Walsh, Mitchell Schechter and Audrey Tischler of the AHSA.
Particular thanks to our editors Anne Becker, Margaret Frith and Nora Cohen.

For Nicole Williamson
L.H.

For Amy Grossman
B.C.

SHOW RIDER

Walking up to the stable at ByWay Farms in the chilly darkness of Christmas Eve, Kerri feels a rush of excitement seeing the weathered old barn glowing with red and green lights. A chime of happy voices fills the night.

"What a great idea to have a party here," Kerri says to her parents and grandmother. Great indeed. What Kerri doesn't know is that everyone in the barn has assembled in her honor.

"Hi, Kerri!" her friends call, greeting her with hugs and kisses.

Kerri weaves her way through the revelers en route to her favorite horse, Cinema I. She notices that many riders have decorated their stalls with evergreens and angel snow. The aroma of freshly baked Christmas cookies mingles with the sweet fragrance of hay, oats and leather.

Kerri has brought Cinema a bag of carrots, hardly traditional Yuletide fare, but, nonetheless the hors d'oeuvre of his choice. In her other hand she carries his present, a plastic feeding bucket purchased with her babysitting money.

Just as she pulls the latch on the stall door, Kerri catches sight of a shiny gold plaque engraved:

CINEMA I
OWNER – KERRI CIBBARELLI

She stares at it bewildered.

"It's for real, Kerri," says her brother, Ed, who is standing behind her.

Slowly, with fingers shaking, Kerri opens the white envelope tacked above the sign.

"Read it to us," calls her good friend Lori.

Kerri draws in her breath. "To our darling Kerri. We hope you are happy with Cinema I. Be as proud of him as we are of you. Care for him and love him. He is very special and he is yours. Love, Mom and Dad."

Kerri can hardly believe her good fortune. Tears fill her eyes. Her face flushes and she runs into the stall to hug Cinema, who is sporting a red Christmas bow tied at a rakish angle around his neck. "I didn't really expect to get a horse. Not ever."

Cinema sweeps his tail back and forth, glowing with the attention. He lowers his head as if to say, "Ah shucks."

At fifteen, Kerri Cibbarelli is an exceptionally talented rider who competes on the horse show circuit. She rides in the Junior Hunter division where the horse's performance is judged, and in Equitation classes where the horsemanship of the rider is judged.

Kerri had been renting Cinema from her instructors, John and Merilee Ventura, for a few months before her parents bought him. To have Cinema for her own was a dream come true.

Cinema is a magnificent chestnut gelding with a coat like satin. He has wide-set brown eyes, ears that perk up showing his keen interest in life and a well proportioned head set on an aristocratic neck. He is strong and bold-looking, measuring 15.3 hands high. Horses are measured in hands rather than feet and inches. A hand is officially defined as 4 inches, the distance across a man's knuckles. The measurement is taken from the highest point of the withers, the ridge between the shoulder blades of a horse, to the ground.

"Kerri had been doing so well with her riding," says her mother Elissa, "we felt she had earned her own horse."

Kerri was not "saddle born" and it came as a surprise to her and her family that riding is her special talent. Many show exhibitors come from "horsey" backgrounds. They are plopped down on pokey old nags while still in diapers. Kerri, by contrast, took her first lesson when she was nine years old. The Cibbarellis live in Holbrook, Long Island, and when Kerri first started riding, her mother took her to Suffolk Farms located nearby.

Kerri at age 10

Kerri performed the exercises with remarkable ease but admits she was a little nervous. "The trainer was a perfectionist. He made me think, but I couldn't get over being scared. See, I was the new kid in the class and everyone was staring at me while I followed his instructions."

After the class, the instructor told Kerri's mother Elissa, "She's a natural."

The first thing the instructor noticed was Kerri's body conformation. Kerri has the right build for an equestrian: long slender legs, a small pelvic region and excellent posture. A slim girl, particularly if she is tall, has a great advantage in the show ring. Short, plump girls do not look well in breeches, the tight elastic pants that riders wear. Their figure faults are displayed when they bounce on top of a graceful animal.

But it isn't just Kerri's build that makes her stand out when she rides. Right from the start, she radiated composure and self-confidence, an air that seemed to say, "I was born to be here."

Riding is a sport that is much more mental than physical. Strength counts, of course. An equestrian needs to draw on a reserve of energy without making it look obvious. But more important, a rider must know how to outsmart her horse, to get him to follow her commands, because there is no way that a human can overpower such a strong animal.

As young as she is, Kerri exhibits another quality crucial for a show rider or any other athlete: determination.

"She has a driving urge to be the best," says her father, Bill. "This is why Kerri does well in the show ring. When it comes to continual testing, Kerri has an edge. This is where many kids fall down. Their minds wander or they don't think show riding is something of overwhelming importance. Kerri has many other interests too—roller disco, reading, skiing, or just being with her friends—but when she's on a horse, she's all business."

At the time Kerri started to ride, she was not sure how far her interests would go. She also wanted to be a competitive swimmer. She hoped to make the team at Sachem, her district school. But on the day of tryouts, Kerri developed aches and a sore throat. Downplaying her symptoms, she told her mother, "I'd like to give it a shot."

As soon as Kerri arrived at the pool she saw the long line of contestants. "I had to wait two hours," remembers Kerri. "When they blew the whistle, I just gave it my all. Even though I felt lousy, I swam the best I could." Her efforts were rewarded; she finished seventh out of 107. When she came home, she climbed in bed with a temperature of 103 and a strep throat.

"You must make a decision," Bill Cibbarelli told his daughter. "If you join the swim team, you'll have to practice six nights a week. That will conflict with riding lessons."

"I kinda like the horses," Kerri responded with a grin.

Today, Bill Cibbarelli shakes his head and smiles at Kerri's expensive choice. "For $29.98 we could have bought her a bathing suit."

The relationship between girls and horses is one of the most intrigu-

ing human bonds. Those who like 'em, love 'em. "I can remember when I was around ten I started to really grow attached to horses," says Kerri. "My friends and I used to play horse show in the backyard. We'd set up a course using chairs turned on their sides or stacks of cushions. Then we'd pretend that we were horses and jump over the obstacles."

Kerri soon discovered she loved horses so much that her riding lesson once a week wasn't enough. Every time she had a free moment, she would say to her mother, "Ma, drive me down to the barn. I want to hang out with the horses."

Kerri made herself useful by feeding the horses, cleaning them, and helping other riders to mount and adjust their stirrups. Her willing nature and adaptability soon earned her the job of exercising horses at Suffolk Farms. By getting on so many mounts, Kerri developed phenomenal versatility for a rider her age. She learned to anticipate a horse's moves and

moods. This is important because equines are temperamental. That's what makes riding so exciting. An athlete who plays tennis or soccer plays with a ball, an inanimate object that isn't going to change from day to day. But with a horse, one morning the animal feels good and the next morning he doesn't. He doesn't want to work quite so hard. His muscles ache a bit here and there. It's the rider's job to get him to perform at the top of his ability.

Show riding seemed the next logical step for Kerri since it would give her something tangible to work for and she would have a chance to test herself against other riders. In her first year of going to horse shows, Kerri moved quickly through the competitive ranks. She started in Maiden, a beginner's division open to riders who have not won a first-place ribbon at a recognized show. In Maiden, the fences are 2 feet high. To a young rider in her first horse show, this is a formidable height, especially when there are several fences. Kerri recalls, "My stomach had butterflies. The fences looked so high to me."

Over a period of time Kerri moved up from Maiden to Novice, a division for riders who have not won three first-place ribbons.

Kerri quickly accumulated a lion's share of ribbons which she proudly displays on her wall of the family den. She was doing so well that Bill and Elissa Cibbarelli switched her to ByWay Farms so she could train with John and Merilee Ventura, instructors who specialize in preparing young people for the advanced show ring.

"Kerri was twelve when she started with us," says Merilee Ventura. "She had a nice soft touch on a horse but needed some polishing. The first thing we worked on was her hands. She cocked her wrists in different directions and it was unappealing to the eye. And she was nippy with the horse's mouth."

With Merilee Ventura

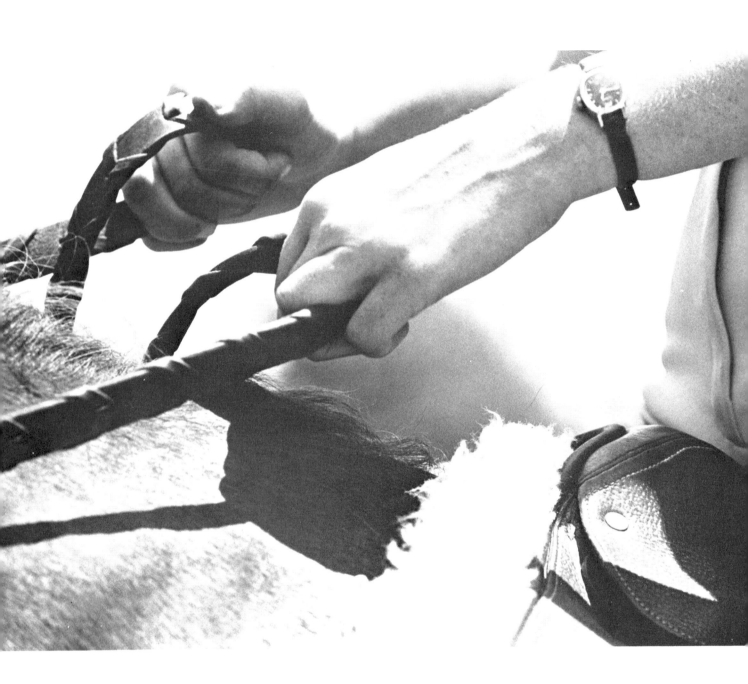

Kerri agrees. "It certainly was my weakness. I'd either be too rough on a horse's mouth or too soft. When I'd get mad I'd jerk on the horse's mouth. I was too hard on him and the judge marked me down."

Some riders carry bad habits with them throughout their careers, faults that started when they were beginners and were not corrected. It was important to John and Merilee Ventura that Kerri be totally schooled before she moved on to more advanced classes. Also, they knew that it is the easiest thing in the world to spoil a horse's mouth and the hardest thing to remake it. A good rider is said to have "good hands" or "light hands," meaning that he or she always has sensitive contact with the horse through the reins or bit.

Despite Kerri's flaws as a fledgling rider, both Merilee and John felt that Kerri had genuine talent backed by good discipline and a willingness to work hard.

Kerri quickly moved into the Limit class, open to horses who have not won six first-place ribbons. Theoretically a rider could enter all these divisions without having won any ribbons, but most don't feel qualified to do so. The next step for Kerri was Open. This class is open to all horses or riders, regardless of winnings. But it is usually only the seasoned riders who choose to enter. An open horsemanship class, however, generally specifies that the rider may be no more than eighteen years old.

Soon Kerri's wall was covered with silver cups and platters, the coveted prizes awarded champions and reserve champions. "What I love about showing," Kerri says, "is that I have a chance to test myself against different horses and different riders. Showing teaches me to be composed under pressure. I have only a few minutes to impress the judge that I am the best in my class."

A few months after Kerri started taking lessons at ByWay Farms, John and Merilee spotted Cinema I at a barn on the east end of Long Island. They discovered that Cinema had been bred as a racehorse and had spent his first years at the track. Since their students compete in horse shows, John and Merilee are always on the lookout for equines who not only are healthy and handsome, but also have the extra strength of character we call personality. A good show horse has charisma, that magnetism which draws people to them. John could see that Cinema I has it in abundance.

Cinema I was four and a half years old, radiating the special glow of a young fit animal. A mix of thoroughbred and quarterhorse, he combines the best of his ancestors. The word thoroughbred stands for the epitome of breeding and elegance. These elites of the horse world are also noted for their competitiveness, high spirits, speed and grace.

From the quarterhorse side of the family, Cinema inherits his solid strength, affectionate disposition and hammy qualities, all so necessary in a show horse. Recalls John, "Cinema looked so glamorous, so special, that I wanted to give him a theatrical name, one that suited a star on the rise. That's why I decided to call him Cinema I."

When John brought Cinema home to ByWay Farms, his first thought was, "He will be a wonderful horse for Kerri and she will be great for him."

The pairing of horse and rider is very important, particularly when the

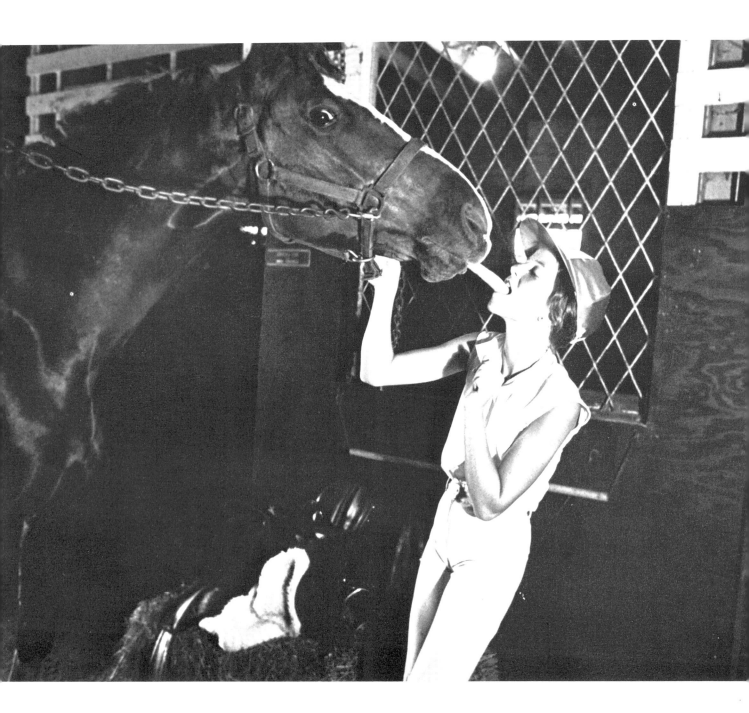

With John Ventura

goal is the show ring. In a sense, the two must marry and then attack a course together. It takes tremendous time, perseverance and technique to school a green horse. And with a horse as young and high-spirited as Cinema, it can also be dangerous. But John knew that Kerri was an even-tempered, controlled rider, not easily shaken, and brave enough to tackle this type of horse.

"It's important to stay on an even keel," says Kerri. "If you get nervous, you trigger nervousness in the horse. You don't want that. So much of the work you do with show horses involves quieting exercises to keep them relaxed."

Many who compete in the show ring ride on "made" horses. These are educated equines who are sold as polished performers. Made horses have been in competition for a number of years and they know what to do. They help train the rider because they are so used to the ring they can just about go around the course without a rider. If a rider has the money, she could conceivably buy a horse in the morning and win a championship in the afternoon. This may not be fair to the people who do their own schooling, but those who do their own schooling and win have a lot more to boast about.

Kerri feels that one of the principal disadvantages of riding a made horse is that the rider does not get the versatility so crucial in the show world. "In some classes the judge will ask us to switch horses. If you've trained on a made horse and you get on a green horse, you won't know how to control the green horse because your made horse doesn't have any problems. He also doesn't provide you with much of a challenge."

When Kerri was first introduced to Cinema, it was not love at first sight. She told John, "He's so rough, so out of control. I can't imagine how he can be turned into a show horse."

Cinema had a bundle of problems which Kerri helped to smooth out. He was frisky and spooked easily. A piece of paper or a loud sound caused him to rear up and buck. Also, Cinema became claustrophobic when he was too close to other horses.

"You need a lot of patience to handle a green horse," says Kerri. "It's like training a kid to walk and talk. I have patience with Cinema but, at home, sometimes I don't. When my dad gets back from work he's tired and he'll say, 'Kerri, will you go upstairs and get my wallet?' or 'Kerri, will you get my keys?' I think to myself, 'I have other things to do besides running around looking for things for him.' Then, later, I'll feel guilty and I'll bring him coffee or I'll just sit with him. I figure, 'Well, he puts up with me when I'm a pain in the neck.' "

Cinema required an extra measure of patience because he was bred for the track, not the show ring. Race horses are worked almost to the point of being neurotic. They are told to do one thing—get out there and run. Show horses must be quiet, alert and responsive. They not only have to be competitive, they also have to know how to keep their composure.

"Self-control is very important in Cinema's case," explains Kerri, "because we are training him to be a hunter rather than a jumper. Most girls are like me. They compete in the Hunter competitions, while the boys prefer the Jumpers. The hunter horse is judged on his style, use of his body and consistency. Hunter showing is supposed to be like the conditions found on a fox hunt. Of course the jumps aren't real, but they are made to look as authentic as possible. The jumps are low and the judge looks for smoothness and grace on the part of the horse. You must control the horse with your hands without looking like you are controlling him.

"In Open Jumper classes, only height and difficulty of jumps are considered. Time is sometimes a factor—a rider cannot exceed the time-allowed limit without incurring penalty points. But as long as the horse's four feet get over the fence and onto the other side, looks and style of horse and rider don't matter."

Kerri was happy to help train Cinema as a hunter since she did not want to jump the bigger fences. "When you go Jumpers, you pretty much ruin a horse for Hunters or Equitation," explains Kerri, referring in the use of the word "equitation" to the show class in which only the horsemanship of the *rider* is judged. "That's because jumpers can act crazy. They are ready to go all the time and they jump really high. Hunters generally jump lower fences."

John agrees with Kerri, "Cinema is a delightful horse. His temperament is suited for Hunters or Equitation because he has a showman's feeling for the subtle nuances of style which these classes require and he has the consistency to perform well over a sustained period of time. Also, if you start a child out on a horse trained for Equitation, a class in which hunters are used, you give them a strong foundation. They can go in any direction. Practically all the riders on the U.S. Equestrian team were equitation riders as juniors."

While John gave Cinema his initial training, it was Kerri's job to school him. They started with the basics. The only two things Cinema could do were walk and run. "If I gave him a little leg," says Kerri, "he would take me on the grand tour."

During workouts, Kerri showed Cinema she was boss, which is not so easy to do when you weigh 95 pounds and the horse weighs 1,200. To establish her primacy, Kerri was clear, definite and firm in her commands. She corrected Cinema if he was disobedient and rewarded him when he acknowledged her authority.

This time-honored method of breaking in a horse works through repetition but, if the horse is frisky, the going isn't smooth. When he would get in the exercise ring, Cinema felt so good, he went to town, bucking his heart out. Kerri was flying out of the saddle and hitting the ground at an alarming rate. Laughs Kerri, "Fortunately I knew how to fall and roll away from the horse."

Schooling Cinema over jumps was a challenge which brought out all of Kerri's equestrian skills. Cinema's first reaction to the fences was to charge them. He grabbed hold of the bit and ran down the jumps, never leaving from the same spot twice and getting over the fences any way he could. It took countless lessons before he learned to recognize and obey Kerri's commands to jump in form, to rise and fall in a smooth arc. Once he did catch on, Kerri's enjoyment of the sheer athletic excitement of riding him was intensified. "Before he got the hang of it, I sometimes used to become so frustrated with him that I'd start to cry."

To get the bucks out of Cinema before riding him and to further his education as a show horse, Kerri embarked on a "longeing" program.

The longe line is a rope about 30 feet long. It is attached to the halter of the horse. Kerri stands beside Cinema's shoulder with the longe line looped in her hand. She asks Cinema to move by clucking her tongue and saying "Walk."

While it is generally a safe procedure, Kerri had one experience with longeing which makes her extra careful. She was longeing a friend's horse, a bold dark bay thoroughbred, when suddenly the animal broke free and headed for the open woods where he might hurt himself. "He was so big," Kerri says, "that I just went flying." Kerri's mother was standing by the open gate and instinctively stretched out her arms like a traffic cop in front of the stampeding animal. He reared to a dead stop.

"Thanks Mom," Kerri called as if this is the sort of thing mothers do every day.

"Don't ask me to do it again," laughed her mother.

While John taught Kerri to school Cinema, Merilee concentrated on her riding form.

"Kerri has a natural seat for riding," says Merilee. The "seat" of a rider means the way she rides, the way she sits in the saddle. There are different seats which a rider may learn. Kerri is learning "hunt" or "hunter seat equitation" because that is the kind of seat used in Hunter and Equitation classes. It is an English style of riding that is used for pleasure riding as well as for showing, hunting and advanced jumping. In the hunt seat, the rider's balance is close to the horse's withers. Thus, her horse is better able to support her weight on its forelegs, while its muscular hind quarters are left free to perform their primary job of propulsion. In the hunt seat, the rider shortens the stirrups enough so she can rise smoothly off the seat by the simple flexing of her ankles, knees, and upper legs. Hunt seat equitation was devised as the most efficient method of enabling a horse to perform certain short-term but intensive activities—racing at full speed and jumping over obstacles.

"A rider's upper body depends entirely on her seat and legs for support," explains Kerri. "You should sit lightly on your horse, arching your back as you stretch your heels down. And always look ahead, in the direction you are going, not down at your hands or at the horse."

After three months of schooling Cinema, Kerri decided to enter him in a horse show. The event was to take place at The Hill, a large riding stable in North Salem, New York. This riding establishment has since been re-named Far West Farms and is presently owned by Joanne Woodward and Paul Newman. Filling out the entry form, Kerri checked off classes in the Equitation and Hunter divisions. She makes the decision about which classes to enter rather than relying on her trainers' or parents' advice. "That independence is good," says Bill Cibbarelli. "We trust her judgment concerning the horse."

The show ring, with all its glamour and excitement, is just the tip of the iceberg. For every minute in the spotlight, hours, days and months of preparation are involved. A good show horse starts with proper care and feeding. The animal needs to look healthy, have a bloom on his coat and a clear, alert eye, and be sufficiently lively and interested in the proceedings to give a responsive ride to his owner.

In order to keep Cinema fit, Kerri schedules visits from Dr. Ruskin McIntosh, Cinema's veterinarian. The doctor gives him checkups and also worms him. "Between visits from the vet," Kerri says, "I use a paste dewormer which I stick in Cinema's mouth with a syringe. It's a kind of medicine that destroys worms in the intestinal tract. He can't stand the taste of it so I always give him apples afterwards."

All animals have worms to some degree. Horses have as many as fifty different kinds which must be kept in check or they can cause trouble. If these parasites are allowed to multiply, they can kill an animal.

Kerri looks forward to visits from Dr. McIntosh because she is considering becoming a veterinarian. "I *think* I could handle it. But I'm not sure because I'm squeamish. I can't stand the sight of blood. And yet, with Cinema, nothing bothers me. I get into his mouth. I clean out his sheath—that's his private parts. Even the smell of the stall doesn't faze me. I'm so wrapped up in him."

Another important part of Cinema's routine is a visit from Hans Schnibble, the farrier. The village blacksmith's shop is gone now. Instead, most farriers have well-outfitted trucks and travel about from stable to stable or farm to farm shoeing horses and tending to minor foot ailments.

The horse's hoof is a complicated structure and it affects the whole equine machine. It bears a far greater load per square inch than the human foot, and the addition of a rider on top is comparable to a man carrying a 40-pound pack. Due to the weight, the horse's feet cannot take a lot of pounding on the ground so often encountered at horse shows, especially during the winter months. Because the hooves are like toenails they continue to grow until they overlap the shoes. "If we grow out of a pair of shoes," Kerri says, "we just get a bigger size. But with a horse, the farrier has to take off the shoes and clip off the excess hooves. He then makes new shoes and fits them to the hooves."

As a show day approaches, Kerri scrutinizes Cinema from teeth to tail. She is aware that there is an aura about consistent winners, a confident glow. And the basic ingredient of that professional look is immaculate grooming of the horse and rider. In his book *Hunter Seat Equitation*, former Olympic rider and top-flight coach George Morris writes: "After all is said and done, a horse in the peak of condition, groomed to perfection, with all the little finishing touches put to an animal for the show ring, has got to be miles ahead of his ragged competition as soon as he enters the ring."

The afternoon before a show, Kerri gives Cinema a brisk workout with a curry comb, which is a round rubber brush with small teeth designed especially for horses' hair. Grooming is not just for cosmetic enhancement. Kerri explains, "After the curry comb, I go to a hard brush to get the dirt off his legs and belly." Regular cleaning of Cinema's skin with vigorous massage and brushing opens up oil and sweat glands which otherwise become clogged with dried sweat, scurf and dirt. Grooming not only removes this material, but also stimulates the oil glands.

With Hans Schnibble

Next, using electric clippers especially designed for horses, Kerri trims Cinema's whiskers as well as the hair around his eyes, ears, fetlocks and coronet areas. She says, "It tidies up the picture and shows off his best features."

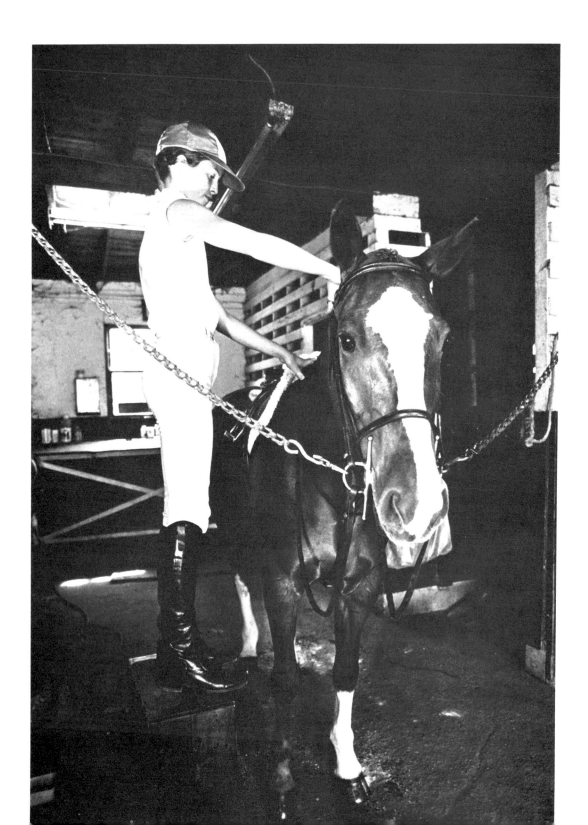

Finally comes the bath. Kerri washes Cinema with human's shampoo, adding creme rinse to his mane and tail which get tangled and matted. She washes him with a large natural sponge and then rinses him with a hose, except for his face which she gently dabs with a wet sponge. Kerri scrapes the excess water off Cinema with an implement designed specially for this purpose. She then slathers his body with Show Sheen. "It's a polish for the hair."

With her mother

Next comes the braiding. Using a crochet hook and bits of tied yarn to keep the strands straight, Kerri does Cinema's mane. Next, she weaves his tail into a sleek French braid. "At first I didn't like to do it because it took so long. But then I started practicing on my own hair and now it takes at most an hour to do Cinema's." To many people, an hour would seem like a long time to spend on just one grooming chore, but not to Kerri. "After all, he's my kid."

Finally she puts cornstarch on Cinema's "socks," as the white hair on his lower legs is called, and she oils his hooves. Standing back from him for a moment, she sighs with satisfaction. "Now, he's really dressed up."

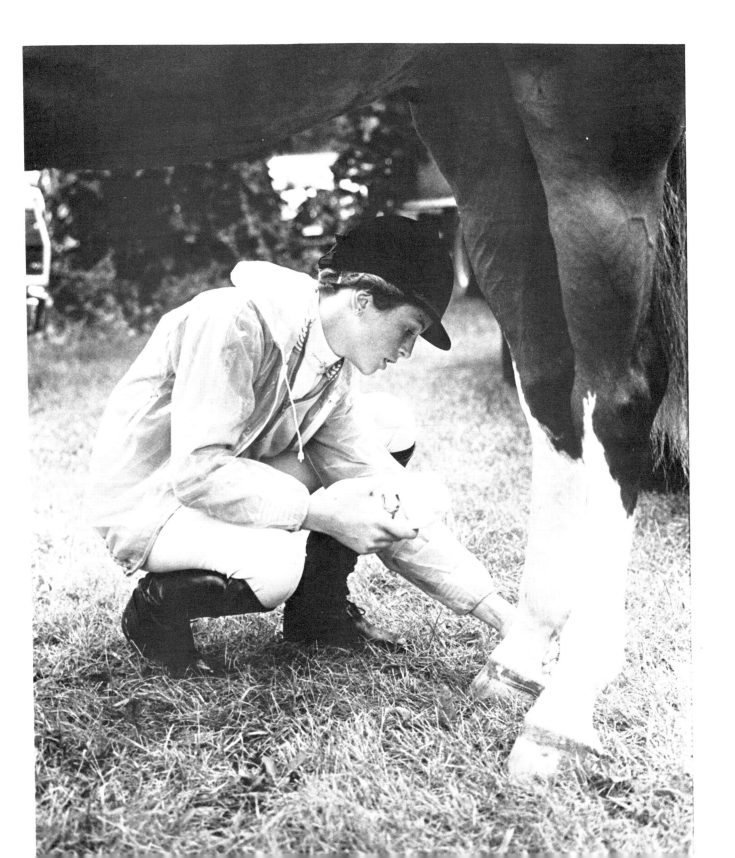

Arriving home from the stable, Kerri takes out her checklist and starts rounding up articles Cinema will need. She uses the front hall as her staging area. She neatly places the articles in her tack trunk, made by her brother Ed. "Let's see," Kerri talks to herself. "I have my fly sheet, tail and leg bandages, grooming kit. Now, where's my saddle soap. Oh, here it is."

Then she sets out her prized possessions, saddle and boots, both of which she has polished to a splendid shine. Kerri has a flat saddle, without extra padding. "Beginner riders have padding in the front part of the saddle to help them ride better. When you get to my level you grip with your knees. It's like skaters who start out with double blades, then when they develop better balance, use single blades."

Kerri's boots are custom-made, cut out of good leather. She wears them each time she rides. "Nobody should wear sneakers," says Kerri. "If you ride in flat shoes, your foot can slide through the stirrup and, if you fall, the horse could drag you."

Next Kerri irons her clothes. The look in the horse world is conservative but smart. For shows, Kerri wears a dark blue fitted jacket, light tan breeches and a "ratcatcher" shirt. Ratcatcher was originally the name of the informal hunting or hacking shirt in England. The word implied that the informal hunter was no better than a hunter of rodents, one who traveled on foot accompanied by a ferret or dog. The ratcatcher shirt is high on the neck and very tight. It has a separate collar with Velcro in the back to hold it on.

Kerri is particularly proud of her shirts which have monograms on them. But what she likes most of all are her gold "snooty fox" earrings. The fox is the mascot for riders and Kerri considers the earrings her good luck charms. "Some judges don't approve of too much jewelry," says Kerri. "I was once marked down for wearing rings on my fingers, so ever since then, I've been careful about that. *But*," she adds with a grin, "I seem to do better with these earrings on."

The judge who marked Kerri down was undoubtedly concerned about safety. One rider broke his finger when a ring he was wearing got caught in the horse's mane and his hand was yanked forward.

The night before a horse show, Kerri goes to bed early. Show days are long, full of waiting, watching, schooling and riding events. She often dreams about the classes. And in these dreams she's always winning. "I see myself taking first place. Sometimes I get so psyched up that it helps me the next day. But I try not to get carried away. If I think 'I'm going to win, I'm going to win,' and I don't win, then I get down."

When Kerri heard the alarm at five o'clock the morning of the Hill show, the adrenalin started racing in her body like a prizefighter responding to the opening bell. Quickly, she got up, showered, combed her hair and tucked it under a net so it wouldn't look messy when she rode. "The net makes me look like an old lady and it embarrasses me when I take my hunt cap off, but it does keep the hair out of my face." Then she rubbed a little gloss on her lips and a touch of blush on her cheeks.

In the crisp October darkness, Kerri led Cinema from the paddock at ByWay Farms into the trailer. Walking slowly, Kerri encouraged him by using a soft voice. She had carefully tied bandages called shipping wraps around his legs and tail so he wouldn't be bruised en route.

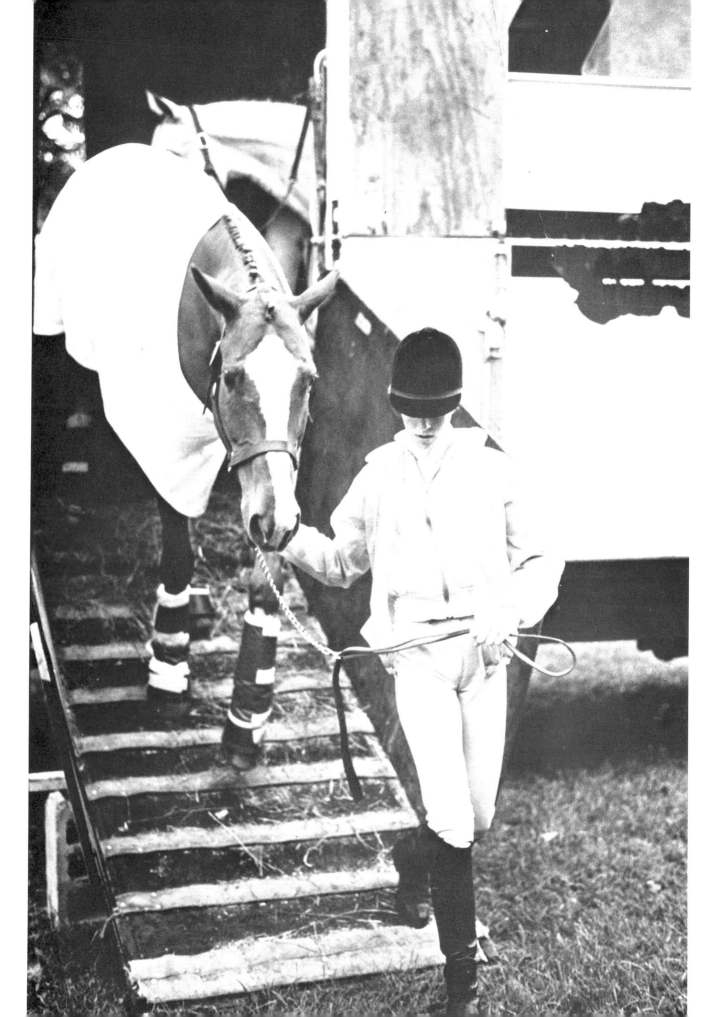

On the way to The Hill, Kerri was calm; she appeared relaxed, organized and unrushed. Sitting behind her mother in the car, though, she betrayed that she was already in the frame of thinking of a show rider. She was a backseat driver, superaware of all the choices her mother must make on the highway. "She has extraordinary peripheral vision," says Elissa Cibbarelli. "It has become so second nature to her to watch out for other horses when she's riding that she is constantly on guard, even in the car."

The pressure started to build for Kerri as soon as she arrived at the show. She was excited, nervous, worried about the different fences and the way they are situated in the show ring. But she didn't show it. She has an actress's gift for projecting confidence—most of the time. A good competitive rider hides her insecurities, just as she finesses her horse's shortcomings when she is in the ring.

While Elissa signed her in at the secretary stand, and picked up her exhibitor's number, Kerri made her way to the ring where she was to have her first class. She passed a schooling ring where a horse was cantering. The rhythm of his hooves could be softly heard. He breathed in and out sharply on the last beat of each stride.

From time to time, Kerri waved hello to other exhibitors, friends she had made from going to horse shows. Most of them are females. The ratio of girls to boys at horse shows is twelve to one.

On the post outside the ring, Kerri studied the course for her first class, Hunter Over Fences. She was looking at an intricate diagram of numbered fences and directional lines depicting the route the riders must take. She committed it to memory, a feat she has become so good at that she can keep the courses for a few classes in her mind at the same time. Kerri then looked at the show ring and ran through the "trip" in her mind. A course is set up in such a way that it challenges both horse and rider and presents fair problems. "Now, let's see," Kerri said to herself. "It's the outside line (meaning fences closest to the rail) to the inside line (fences on the inner part of the ring), to the diagonal line, to the outside line again . . ."

Sometimes if Kerri is unsure of a course, she will walk it so that she can pace Cinema's strides to be in the right place when he takes off. Hunters are supposed to move with long, flat strides. Explains Kerri, "A horse has to be a really good mover to get to the top. That's what is exciting about Cinema. He moves beautifully."

After practicing over jumps in the schooling area, Kerri tied her number, 186, around the back of her jacket and took a warm-up class. This is like a dress rehearsal. "You should always have a warm-up class," says Kerri. "This way you get your horse to see the fences before your regular class." She was now ready for her class.

While Kerri waited her turn, she evaluated the riders who went before her. She looked at them as a riding instructor would, asking herself about the pacing of their strides. "If the fences are far apart, I say to myself, 'Steady five?' This means that a rider should slow down between jumps." She digests this material quickly so that when she goes over the same course she might have a better trip.

"Kerri Cibbarelli, Number 186," the announcer called. A look of concentration settled over Kerri's face; Cinema, who loves the show ring, also became more alert.

"As the horse in front of me is exiting," explains Kerri, "I do last minute fixings, such as adjusting my stirrups or tightening my girth. I enter the ring at a trot making my circle to pick up the canter. I am moving up to the right pace for the first fence. Now, I say to myself, 'Do I have to move forward—make Cinema go faster—for this spot or stay steady?' The first fence is important because it sets the rhythm for the trip. As I come into the fence I look through it to see the landing position. At the same time I am careful to concentrate on my lower legs, heels and my elbows, making sure they aren't flapping out. I keep a picture in my mind of the ideal jump position as I go over. That's one down, seven more to go."

Coming around the turn after the first fence, Kerri tried to get her "flying change" of lead. When a horse is asked to change from one lead to another at a canter without coming to a trot or reducing his gait, he is said to be doing a flying change. Explains Kerri, "Cinema's leg which is closest to the center of the ring should be his leading leg. So each time he changes direction, he should change his lead too. It takes a lot of practice to get a horse to do this in a way that looks natural.

"If the next two jumps are on an outside line, I again say to myself, is it steady or moving forward? I encourage the horse forward. If he's going too fast, I say, 'Ho.' If he's too slow, I 'cluck' or squeeze with my legs. The last fence is the tough one because I have a tendency to let down. I think, 'It's almost over.' To keep my momentum, I pretend that there are at least two more fences after the last fence."

After all the exhibitors had finished their rounds, Kerri heard the magic words over the loudspeaker: "First Place, Kerri Cibbarelli." With that, Kerri jogged Cinema to the middle of the ring and accepted a blue ribbon from the ringmaster. "Cinema loves to win," says Kerri. "He looks so proud whenever we pin. He also knows when he loses. He drops his head and mopes until the next class."

Kerri now prepared for the Equitation class which is usually the most popular event at the show. Sometimes it will draw as many as seventy-five riders. Says Kerri: "In Equitation, the horse's performance is not really judged. It's the rider's position, form and ability to make the horse perform on command."

In this event, Kerri is careful to make her position as near-perfect as she can. "I straighten up, pushing my weight into my heels. Then I tighten my calf muscles to make better contact with the horse. By arching my back, it helps me get a better feel with the reins."

Despite "chipping" a fence, Kerri came in sixth, which was better than she expected to do. A chip means that Cinema came too close to the fence and hesitated because Kerri had shortened his strides too much. He may or may not have actually touched the fence but, in either case, there was a momentary break in the flow of his jump.

John was waiting just outside the gate, ready to analyze Kerri's performance. He always tells Kerri what she did wrong right away so Kerri won't dwell on it. Often his on-the-spot evaluation is unnecessary because Kerri has already figured out where she goofed. John acknowledges, "She's her own toughest critic."

After four classes in the afternoon, Cinema had had it. He parked his head on Kerri's shoulder for a quiet snooze.

On the way home, Kerri followed Cinema's example and rested her head on her brother Ed's shoulder. Slouched in the back of the Cibbarellis' Grand Prix, Kerri's body was limp and numb with exhaustion. Still, bright spots of the day floated through her mind as she played with the ribbons in her hand.

"Sometimes Kerri is so tired that she has to drag herself to school on Monday mornings," says Elissa, who doesn't worry if Kerri has an off day every now and then because Kerri is a B-plus student. "If her rounds at shows are scattered throughout the day, she puts in twelve hours. It's not like an ice skating competition where a girl can take off her skates and go out for lunch. Kerri must stay dressed and be near Cinema all day long. She is either feeding him, schooling him or cooling him off."

With her mother and father

Horse shows are not only draining for Kerri, they are also tiring for the Cibbarellis who stand on the sidelines giving moral support. Despite a demanding job with the Bell System, Bill Cibbarelli has only missed a couple of horse shows in the five years Kerri has been competing.

Showing horses is expensive as well as time-consuming. The maintenance of a horse like Cinema I costs the Cibbarellis as much per year as the care and feeding of both their children. The boarding of Cinema plus the expenses for tack, blacksmith and vet fees come to about $4,500 a year. In addition, each show costs on the average $80, depending on how many events Kerri enters. Renting a trailer can cost from $20 to $40 for local shows, more for long-distance trips. Add to this the cost of riding lessons and coaching. Taking into account all these expenses, horse showing runs about $10,000 to $12,000 a year for competition on the local level, and considerably more if the horse and rider travel to the big shows.

"We have to make sacrifices," says Bill Cibbarelli. "Everybody in the family has to really want it for her. A friend will sometimes ask, 'Why put up with all this expense when another sport, say track or swimming, would cost a fraction of participating in the horse show world?' I tell them it's because this is what Kerri wants and she has shown us that she has exceptional talent as an equestrian. I don't want her to be thirty-five and watching a Grand Prix jumper and saying, 'What if?' "

Elissa nods her head in agreement. "We encouraged her. We backed her up. How do you stick something in front of somebody and then after two or three years say, 'Hey! This is getting to be too much' and take it away from her?"

In her small way, Kerri contributes to the family income by babysitting and using gift-money to buy necessities for Cinema. When she was only ten years old, she looked after twin infants. Their mother had such faith in Kerri that she wouldn't leave them with any other sitter. Now Kerri looks after a neighbor's eighteen-month-old boy. He adores Kerri and loves it when she takes him for rides on Cinema.

Kerri enjoys babysitting, just as she takes great pleasure in looking after Cinema, as well as other animals. Her affection for equines has made her very popular at the barn. Other riders can always count on Kerri to exercise their horses if they can't make it to the barn.

As soon as Kerri got home from The Hill, she ran her dirty riding clothes through the washing machine and carefully put away her saddle, riding gear and trunk in a small tack room off the family den.

Later in the evening, Kerri was still too geared up from the horse show to fall asleep. She wandered over to Ed's room where she announced her presence by hanging on the chinning bar screwed on just outside his door.

Ed is sixteen and values his privacy. At the moment Kerri intruded, he was talking to his friend on the phone. He did not appreciate Kerri's unannounced visit.

"Ohoooo," hummed Kerri, swinging back and forth on the bar. "Ed's got a girlfriend."

"Kerri, get out of here."

"No. I want to listen."

Ed closed the door on Kerri, who, still hanging, waited silently for a few moments. Then, just when Ed had settled back into his conversation, Kerri kicked the bedroom door open and laughed, "I heard every word you said."

Despite these fleeting moments when Ed would like to ship Kerri off to Outer Mongolia, they are very close. Ed faithfully attends Kerri's horse shows, urging bystanders to cheer when she enters the ring.

Sailing is Ed's sport, and in the summers, he will take Kerri out in his *Sunfish* on Long Island Sound. For all Kerri's equestrian bravery, she becomes a submissive crewmember on her brother's boat. If Kerri is steering and the water gets choppy, she gives the tiller to Ed. "Kerri is afraid of making a mistake," says Ed. "If she made a booboo and flipped the boat over, she would feel that I would never let her live it down."

"He's right!" says Kerri.

Most days Kerri eagerly looks forward to exercising Cinema, a routine which takes at least two hours a day. She usually does it after school or, when school's out, she does it in the mornings. But in the winter, when it's icy, windy and bitter cold, Kerri would rather be inside snuggled up next to a warm fire. "It's no fun riding in the dark in sub-freezing weather.

Particularly at the horse shows where there's a lot of waiting around. I remember one show at Suffolk Farms where it was zero degrees and so cold that the judge said, 'Forget the posted jumping order. Whoever's ready, go.' The riders crowded at the entry gate, so I decided to do a little more schooling. By the time I finished, my nose, ears and toes felt as if they were frostbitten. It didn't hurt all that much when I was outside but when I got warm and started to thaw out, it was murder."

It always seems to be on the frigid, bone-chilling, damp days that Cinema decides to give himself a squishy, dirty bath on the ground, which means that Kerri must spend hours drying him off so he won't catch pneumonia. "Cinema's a mud lover," explains Kerri. "Show him a puddle and he'll roll in it. And he always picks the muddiest days to throw me off."

One of Kerri's persistent fears is that, because Cinema becomes very aggressive when turned out in the paddock, he will hurt himself. Since Cinema has too much energy to spend all his time in the stall and Kerri can ride him for only two or three hours a day, he must spend some unsupervised time romping about with the other horses in the paddock.

Kerri's dark worry came true one day when she walked into Cinema's stall and saw a large gash on his leg. The area around his hock looked very bad; all the skin was torn off. The hock is the elevated protruding region of the hind limb of a horse. This joint, and the muscles and tendons which sheathe it, carry a great deal of the horse's working load. A horse "jumps from his hocks." That is, he receives the necessary spring and propulsion from this joint. If the hock is weak, he will have trouble lifting himself over fences.

Kerri called Dr. McIntosh and he cleaned the wound and gave Kerri instructions on how to care for it. The injury would require a lot of attention. Neither Kerri nor anyone at the barn had a clue how it happened. Later, when she told her family about it, her dad and brother offered to take over the 11:00 P.M. changing of the dressing.

After a few weeks, Kerri felt that Cinema was well enough to ride in competition. At the Mid-Island show, after a successful jumping trip, she entered the ring to do a flat equitation class. In this class she was asked to back the horse, to do a figure eight at a trot and a canter, and to hand gallop and halt.

Kerri's flatwork was smooth. She was careful to give Cinema just enough control in the hands and legs to ensure a fluid performance. When the judge called for additional testing, Kerri was among the finalists summoned. She was thrilled to make the cut because the competition was stiff.

While Kerri was cantering as part of the test, the horse in front of her suddenly kicked up his rear leg, hitting Cinema and whacking Kerri in the ball of the foot, causing her to fall off. "I landed on my feet but my first worry was that Cinema might have been seriously hurt."

"Numbers 118 and 145 leave the ring," said the judge, eliminating both the girl whose horse did the kicking and Kerri because she fell off.

The judge felt as bad as Kerri. Later he told Merilee, "It's too bad, her fence position was the best out there."

Cinema's injury was minor but with the onset of winter, the weather became brutal. Kerri decided to keep him off the horse show circuit for a while. "When spring comes, he'll be in top condition," she said with hope in her voice.

Then, one day in February, the weight of the worry about Cinema started to get to Kerri. What if Cinema is a bad luck horse? What if he has another injury? Kerri knew a girl whose parents sold her horse because the animal had a bum leg.

That evening, Kerri told her mother her fears. "I don't ever want to give up Cinema. I want to work out our problems together."

"Oh, Kerri," Elissa said. "Cinema is yours. He'll always belong to you. Even when you go off to college, we won't sell him to pay your tuition. He's yours forever."

By the time spring came, both Kerri and Cinema had profited from their rest from the show circuit. They were physically sound, eager to compete and ready to conquer. Appropriately, the setting was perfect for victory.

Of all the horse shows on Long Island, Caumset is the most beautiful location. This equestrian park on the North Shore of Long Island had been the home of the Marshall Field family, the department store heirs, until they made a gift of it to New York State. The park is replete with bridle paths, carefully manicured lawns and freshly painted paddocks. The young competitors add to the attractive sight. They swirl and turn their horses and take the waiting practice fences under the critical gaze of their mentors who stand in informal groups along the rail.

This show was crucial for Kerri because she was riding in the Mini-Medal and Mini-Maclay divisions for the first time. The "Minis" are simplified versions of the Medal and Maclay categories, the toughest competitions on the horse show program. The Minis are stepping-stones to help the riders work up to the top categories. The basic difference between the Minis and the actual Medal and Maclay classes is that, in Minis, the fences are 3 feet instead of 3 feet 6 inches.

Both Medal and Maclay classes include intricate jumping courses and special tests of an advanced nature. The tests are even harder for those lucky contestants who are good enough to reach the finals. The Medal class is sponsored by the American Horse Shows Association and the finals are held in Harrisburg, Pennsylvania, each year. To qualify, riders in Kerri's part of the country must win four blue ribbons. The Medal classes are held over a figure eight course with two changes of direction. Of the original group, four to six riders are called back to do at least two additional tests. These tests can include changing horses, trotting jumps or jumping without stirrups.

The Alfred B. Maclay finals, sponsored by the American Society for the Prevention of Cruelty to Animals, are held every November at Madison Square Garden. This event also requires qualifying by winning four blue ribbons (in Kerri's region of the nation). In this competition, the riders are required to do a course over fences and wait for a call back to do a thorough workout on the flat. Since flat work counts for fifty percent, the rider's flat work had better match her proficiency over fences or she's out of luck. The judging for both events is tough and competitive. Over the years many Medal and Maclay winners have gone on to become Olympic riders or top professional trainers. "I think the Medal is more difficult because of the tests," says Kerri. "But there's more prestige attached to the Maclay because the finals competition is held at Madison Square Garden in New York."

As the events of the day got underway, Kerri's optimism seemed justified. She won the warm-up class, which means that she pinned blue but no points were given that could be counted against year-end awards. It was the first event of the day, which attracted fifty-three exhibitors. She then went on to pin first place in both Mini-Medal and Mini-Maclay. Each class had over forty riders.

As Kerri left the ring following the Mini-Maclay class, she caught a glimpse of a fellow rider who looked upset. She was giving water to her horse.

"What's the matter?" Kerri asked.

"My horse stopped at a fence and I fell off and crashed through the rails. She's really been giving me a rough time. For the past month she's been stopping at the fences."

Kerri knew this competition was important to her friend. She was a more advanced rider than Kerri and this was her year to qualify for Madison Square Garden. If she could pin here, it would help her chances of making it to the Garden in November. Looking at her now, Kerri could see the worry in her eyes.

"I'll lend you Cinema," Kerri said, knowing full well that she would have to drop out of two classes she was hoping to post-enter. Since she had triumphed in the Minis, she was thinking of giving Medal and Maclay a try. They were also held at Caumset on this day. But the rules say there can be only one rider per horse in each class. If someone else rode Cinema, Kerri would have to bow out.

Kerri's generosity was her friend's good fortune. Kerri stood on the sidelines and cheered as her friend took third place in the Maclay.

Later, Bill Cibbarelli told Kerri, "I'm very proud of you. You showed the true spirit of sports competition."

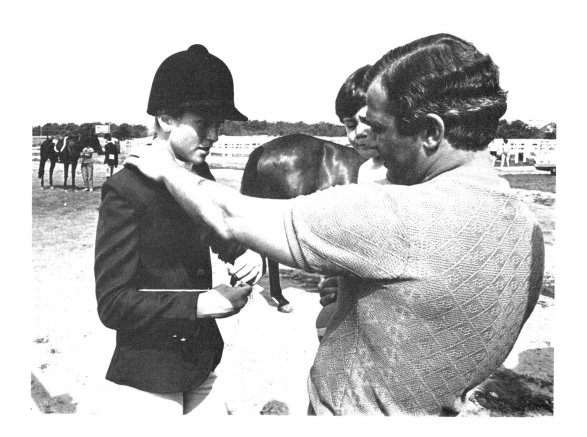

As it turned out, Kerri was not only a winner in terms of character, she also walked away with the title of Champion for the Junior Amateur Owner division. This award is granted for cumulative points won in that division during the course of this show.

By the time Kerri entered the ByWay Farms show in the beginning of May, she felt invincible, as if each horse show would bring fresh laurels.

Kerri was doing fine until she entered the Junior Hunter Class. As she rounded the first two fences, her rhythm was smooth and steady. But as she came around to the third fence, which had an indentation in front of it, Cinema came to an abrupt stop. This is known in the show world as a refusal, or colloquially as a "dirty stop."

Kerri felt her body shake and numbness set in. In panic, she looked over to John who was watching from the rail. She saw him move his arm in a broad circle, indicating that she should approach the fence once more.

When John signals to Kerri in this way, he knows that she is already out of the running but he wants to teach Cinema a lesson. A "stopper" should always be punished. A refusal to jump a fence, for whatever reason, is a serious disobedience and must be treated as such.

Kerri leaned forward, putting a little extra pressure on her legs. Then she hit Cinema with her stick. Once again he stopped. Unable to hold in her feelings any longer, Kerri's eyes filled with tears. Then quickly, she regained control of herself and came around a third time. At last Cinema jumped the fence.

Coming out of the ring, Kerri darted away from the crowd so the spectators wouldn't see her tears. As she wiped her face, her mother ran up to her.

"Kerri. Don't be so hard on yourself," Elissa told her. "Just to go out there and perform in front of a whole group of people takes a lot of guts."

Kerri was disappointed. "Cinema stopped on me," Kerri said, still totally confused by what had just happened. Then, quickly, Kerri realized that she was doing something which she never permits herself to do. She was blaming Cinema. The responsibility for a trip is the rider's and Kerri knew she was passing the buck. She had caused her horse to make a serious mistake and she had to find out why.

During her next schooling lesson, following the setback at ByWay Farms, John explained to Kerri: "You need more mileage, that's all. Most of the riders you are competing against have at least two years more experience than you do. The more you ride and perfect your form, the fewer mistakes you'll make."

John concentrated on Cinema's dirty stop. He came down hard on

Kerri, breaking the incident into its components, but he was careful not to make it personal because he knew that at that moment Kerri's ego was fragile.

Cinema spooked at the fence because he saw the small ditch in front of it; his natural reaction was to stop rather than jump. Kerri must steer Cinema into the jump at such an angle that his instincts tell him to go forward over it. This is called finding a spot. Four or five strides before a fence, Kerri has to decide either to keep steady or go forward to get the right take-off point. That take-off point is the spot she is looking for.

In order to master finding a spot, Kerri must work on eye control. In the show ring, when the rider is coming toward the fence, she must look at the fence and choose a line, then judge the distance to the fence.

Riders must also practice looking at a predetermined point on the far side of the jump. Otherwise, they fall into the habit of dropping their eyes, looking down as they go over the top of the fence. This causes the rider to duck, to drop her weight to one side of the horse or the other, which in turn throws the horse's balance off.

By the time the St. Joseph's show rolled around two weeks later, Kerri was still apprehensive. She was riding too conservatively, trying to anticipate any mistakes. "There has to be a confident rhythm to a round," explained Merilee. "This is so you can take the horse forward and back. Since Kerri is fearful, she is getting Cinema too close to the fences. He has limited options when jumping from a close spot. He could crash a fence."

At the St. Joseph's Academy Show she competed for prizes in a category called First Year Green which is restricted to horses of any age who are in their first year of showing. This category is almost exclusively made up of professional riders.

A "Pro" in the show world is a competitor over eighteen years old who rides horses for money. Pros often ride horses for owners who are interested in having their equines shown with the idea of selling them. This day Kerri was the only Junior in the division and she pinned a second and third place and was awarded the Reserve Champion ribbon along with $160. (In the Hunter division, Juniors are allowed to accept money on behalf of their horses.) This is an extraordinary achievement for someone Kerri's age. Since she pinned in this division, Kerri qualified for entry in the Citibank Gold Hunter Class. She earned sixth place in this class and received a $50 gold piece.

Through the summer, Kerri competed in shows. Some of them were fun outings, such as Sagaponack which is near the ocean. After Kerri finished her rounds there, she put on her bathing suit and took a long bareback ride on Cinema along the wide sandy beach. But many shows were real tests of endurance for Kerri. She sometimes got light-headed from exercising so strenuously in the heat. July shows such as Holbrook, located in the middle of Long Island, far from the shore, were dustbowls. On each round, Kerri got dirt in her ears, her lungs, on her clothes and in her hair. The temperature climbed in the 90's. Even Cinema turned mopey. "It's silly to complain about the conditions," says Kerri. "They're the same for everyone."

It was at the Holbrook show that Kerri ran into a familiar face.

"Hi, Mr. Walsh," Kerri said with a wide smile.

Jim Walsh, the show steward, tipped his hat to Kerri in a mock gesture

With Jim Walsh

of courtliness. The horse show steward is seldom seen or heard from in the ring, yet his role is vital to every exhibitor. He is the official spokesman for the American Horse Shows Association (AHSA), the governing organization which licenses shows throughout the United States.

The steward is responsible for the correct conduct of the show and he assists in settling questions about personal attire, about class specifications, and about eligibility in a particular event. If an exhibitor wishes to speak to the judge, he must first get permission from the steward. If an exhibitor wants to file a protest, the steward is the person to see.

Jim Walsh also tries to bring the philosophy of the American Horse Shows Association to the shows. "Too many exhibitors think it's a matter of life and death if they pin or not," Jim says. "Not everyone can be a champion and that's not the reason for these shows. The purpose is to have fun and to learn qualities of character such as discipline and responsibility." Then he adds: "I like to see riders with Kerri's attitude. She dotes on her horse, but she also knows that other things are important. Riders shouldn't think of this as an end in itself. They ought to look ahead to going to college and broadening their horizons."

Before Kerri realized it, summer was drawing to a close and the dates of two important horse shows in her area—the Hampton Classic and the Long Island Classic—were approaching.

Horse shows are divided mainly into three categories: *A*, *B*, and *C*. The amount of money awarded and the number and variety of the classes are the bases used for determining whether a show is *A*, *B* or *C*. The *A* shows are top of the line, lasting three or four days and attracting the best riders and horses from all parts of the country. *B* shows are usually one-day affairs and considerably less competitive. The *C* shows are even smaller. Additionally, there are local shows that have no rating but are members of the AHSA. These tend to attract beginners and can be a great deal of fun. With *A* and *B* shows, the points for Medal and Maclay count equally, regardless of the category of the show, as long as it is recognized by the AHSA. The Hampton Classic is an elegant *A* event and also one of the biggest horse shows in the country. This year there will be 934 exhibitors and about 20,000 spectators.

Filling out the entry form, Kerri decided to enter only three events. This was her first year at the Classic and she knew the competition would be stiff. To have a bad trip at the Hampton Classic would be disappointing because the show was filled with gifted riders. "I'll enter in the Hunter classes and stay away from Equitation," Kerri decided. "I want to get my feet wet in the classes I feel most comfortable in."

Three weeks later, arriving at Dune Alpin Farm, the site of the Hampton Classic, located on Montauk Highway, just outside of East-hampton, Kerri's head turned left and right, trying to take in the whole spectacle at once. The grounds looked like a scene from the court of King Arthur. Banners flew from tent poles, and, in the schooling rings, magnificent horses practiced their jumping. Many world famous riders had come to enter Grand Prix jumping events. The Grand Prix is the most prestigious of the 150 riding events at the Classic, drawing riders from all across the United States, Canada, Mexico, Ecuador and England. In this event the riders make impossible-looking turns to truly enormous fences, putting in breathtaking rounds.

Passing a schooling ring, Kerri spotted Melanie Smith, one of the leading show jumping riders in the world. Melanie, who rode only bare-

With Melanie Smith

back until she was twelve, was a member of the United States Equestrian Team's Gold Medal-winning team at the 1979 Pan-American Games in Puerto Rico. With five major Grand Prix victories in 1978, Melanie earned the 1978 Grand Prix Rider-of-the-Year Award, as well as the Leading Lady Rider; her mount Val de Loire took Horse-of-the-Year honors. When Melanie started riding Val de Loire, he refused to jump fences, but through loving attention and strict training, she turned him into a champion. Then they both started to take home ribbons. In 1982, Melanie won the World Cup in Sweden. Says Melanie, "Winning never gets old."

In one class, Local Hunter Over Fences, Kerri handled Cinema well, though they didn't place. But when she entered Local Hunter Under Saddle, which is a flat class, Kerri's competitive instincts surfaced and she pinned blue.

Something particularly nice about winning at a big show is the applause of the crowd. Several of the girls from ByWay Farms, with whom Kerri is friends, were there at the Classic. They crowded around her, congratulating her performance.

Feeling jubilant, with no more classes for the day, Kerri roamed the grounds. Near the ABC television tower, set up to film the event, Kerri saw one of the most colorful personalities in the horse show world.

He is Harry DeLeyer, famous rider of jumpers, who's known for his go-for-broke style. He's called the Galloping Grandfather. In his sixties, Harry still competes on jumpers at Madison Square Garden. He is a familiar sight to Garden spectators. After he finishes the jumping course, he tosses his hunt cap in the air and catches it with his other hand, showing the audience the pink bald spot on his scalp. He often accepts a ribbon with his little grandchild on his lap.

Harry DeLeyer is a prime example of one of the pluses of horse show competition. This is a sport which offers competitive enjoyment for most of a person's life. A high-level gymnast can be finished at twenty, a swimmer at twenty-five, a ballet dancer at thirty-five and a tennis player at forty. "I want to be an image to young people," says Harry DeLeyer. "They say, 'Look at this old man ride. Look at him do it.' Well, I hope they

With Harry DeLeyer

copy me in years to come and they are ten times more successful than I am, but I hope they do it in the right way." Harry knows that some riders get so caught up in chasing ribbons that they forget that riding is a sport in which the fun comes from mastering skills.

While the Hampton Classic represented the most glamorous horse show Kerri attended all year, the Long Island Classic was the most challenging. Here, at the end of the first week in September, she competed in the finals for the Mini-Medal and Mini-Maclay.

Kerri knew she would be riding against tough company. "Everybody who was there had to qualify by pinning first or second in the Minis at other shows," Kerri says. "It was the best riding against the best."

When Kerri didn't place in the Mini-Medal class, she told herself, "I still have a shot at Mini-Maclay and I'm really going to go for it."

As she entered the ring, Kerri realized that she was uncommonly nervous. She could feel herself momentarily sliding back into her old faults, letting her hands nip the reins in an effort to control Cinema. Then the butterflies disappeared. The first two fences were smooth and elegant. There was a fighting chance that this could be a first-class trip. "C'mon Cinema. We can do it," Kerri urged him on, saying the words to herself, while showing the world an outward pose of control.

Going into the third fence, Cinema was slightly off his stride and he chipped it. Kerri realized that in the company of forty-five good riders, this fault was serious enough to put her out of the running.

Kerri finished the run without another flaw, being careful not to let her face show her disappointment.

"You looked marvelous," a friend called to Kerri, not realizing the importance of the chip.

"I did terribly," Kerri said, revealing a temporary lack of composure. One of the hardest things about losing is that people crowd around you almost as much as when you win, and you have to put on a brave face.

Two hours later Kerri pinned high in two fence classes and one flat class. She won the championship for Local Hunter.

One of the most frustrating aspects of showing is that so much depends on opinion. A given judge at a given time may differ totally from another one somewhere else, making it quite unlike a race, where the first past the post is always the winner. Showing is more like participating in a piano competition in which each contestant is given the same sonata to play. The winner is chosen on the basis of finesse of execution.

Penny Rosenthal, one of the leading judges on Long Island who also judges nationwide, explains how she evaluates a horse's performance: "My theory is that anything I *see* is wrong. In other words, horse and rider should present a relaxed, harmonious picture. If I see a loose leg or, in a Hunter class, a horse who gets too close to the fence, then I've seen an out-of-harmony picture. I am looking for my idea of a 'perfect trip' and the rider who comes closest in a particular class on a particular day wins."

Judges use a codified system, a shorthand method of dots, dashes and stickmen to make quick notes about a rider's performance. By minimizing the time the judge has to write, it ensures that he or she will have more opportunity to survey the show ring and assess the merit of each rider.

The judges' individual opinions come in when they decide how much emphasis they will put on various aspects of the rider's performance or a horse's physical characteristics. Some judges like a bold-looking hunter. Other judges prefer softer horses, ones that have an easy flow to their

With Penny Rosenthal

movements. Penny Rosenthal doesn't mind if riders carry a stick in a class but she doesn't like to see bats and crops used excessively. She wants riders to use their natural aids such as legs and feet. Another judge might not mind a slight use of the whip.

Perhaps Kerri's greatest victory this year is not the triumphs at Caumset, St. Joseph's Academy or the Hampton Classic, but the fact that she has learned to handle defeat and disappointment. She's a seasoned competitor who has built her skills on a solid foundation. "I don't give up easily," Kerri says. "I just keep on trying."

This coming year Kerri will work on that extra touch, the theatrical. It's the frosting on the cake. Top riders know how to incorporate the basics, showing them to the judge in the most subtle way, creating the mildest, softest, most fluid picture. Riding is like dancing. It's a matter of bringing together rhythm, balance, tone and line in a sophisticated way.

Up until this point in her riding career, Kerri has been given the time and training to progress at a slow, steady rate. She is now beginning a campaign which, if successful, will take her to Madison Square Garden this year or next. So the momentum speeds up. She must be five times as good a rider as she has ever been. This coming year she will be going to two or maybe three shows a weekend and her hours of instruction will be greatly increased.

Qualifying for the National Horse Show at Madison Square Garden is itself prestigious. In Kerri's area, a rider must have earned four blue ribbons within the year. In other parts of the country, a rider needs just three, two or one blue ribbon to qualify. This may not seem like much but the competition is extremely stiff. Only approximately fifty hunters with the highest scores nationwide are accepted in the Maclay division and the finalists are whittled down to fifteen.

Many of the people who compete for the Garden are so eager to qualify for the Junior Hunter Division and the Maclay finals that they adopt a gypsy life in pursuit of ribbons. The *A* circuit begins in Florida in February and runs until the beginning of October. Riders hop from state to state, working their way north through the Carolinas and Virginia, and then make a lateral migration to the fashionable Grosse Point, Michigan, and

With Rita Tempanaro

Oak Brook, Illinois, shows. They live out of suitcases, in vans and motel rooms, or commute to the showgrounds by airplane, frantically trying to get their school homework done in flight.

Many experts feel that a junior must show under the supervision of a top professional coach such as George Morris, Victor Hugo-Vidal, Ronnie Mutch or Paul Valliere, in order to qualify for the Garden. The top pros have the expertise to train both horse and rider to be physically fit, emotionally cool and mentally fresh enough to meet the demands of weekly, high-level competition.

Knowing the kind of competition she will be up against, Kerri and her parents decided to switch her to Joy Farms where she now trains under Medal winner Rita Tempanaro. "Rita's a gut rider," says Kerri. "She understands the butterflies, the churning in the stomach."

Rita lived out Kerri's dream of going to the big shows when she was quite young. She qualified for Madison Square Garden when she was only twelve years old. She came in second in the Maclay when she was thirteen and took first place at Harrisburg in the Medal. In all, she went to the Medal finals five times and the Garden five times. "I wanted it very much," says Rita. "I would die if I couldn't ride for a day." Rita is very happy to have Kerri as a student. "It's rare to find a rider as focused as Kerri," Rita says. "She's one hundred percent tuned into what she is doing and she's not afraid to make decisions at fences. The hesitaters never make it to the top in this sport."

Rita has a well-thought-out game plan to qualify Kerri for the Garden. In addition to working with her on Cinema, she is having Kerri ride other horses at the barn to increase her flexibility. And she is also expanding Kerri's world. Now Kerri will go to more *A* shows, such as the three- and four-day events at OxRidge in Connecticut and the Devon Horse Show in Pennsylvania. "I don't want her just to *go* to the finals," says Rita. "I want her to *win* and to do this she needs experience going up against the best."

Often the "best" have more potential because they can afford top quality stock. Ten percent of the horses win ninety percent of the classes. Hunters who go to the Garden can cost as much as $75,000 to $150,000.

These formidable statistics do not faze Kerri. "I'm glad my parents didn't buy me a 'made' horse because I enjoy the challenge of training a green horse. It gets me closer to him."

Kerri feels she has a very good chance to make it to the Garden. But if she doesn't qualify this year, it won't be so bad, because, in a way, she's achieving her goal right now. She is having fun doing the thing she loves.

"Winning is great," says Kerri, "but it's not all. The thrill is also preparing Cinema to go into the ring."

Kerri and Cinema have both matured. They trust each other now. It's almost like two kids growing up together. They are comfortable together and take great pleasure in each other's company.

Kerri can be just as happy riding Cinema in the beautiful cross country trails at Joy Farms as she is at the Hampton Classic. "I can go at a gallop and let all my frustrations out or just mosey along in the woods or on the trail down by the lake. Riding is a sport you do with a living thing. A horse may not be a person but he sure has a personality. Cinema is my best friend."

GLOSSARY

Aids—Devices used by the rider to control and guide the horse. *Natural aids* are the rider's hands, legs, back, voice and distribution of weight (equilibrium). *Artificial aids* include reins, martingales, bats and spurs.

American Horse Shows Association (AHSA)—The most widely known horse show organization in the United States. Many of our major shows today are held under its auspices. The AHSA publishes a rule book and a listing of names and stewards throughout the country.

Breeding—The action or process of bearing or generating. Breeding with regard to horses often means controlled mating for the propagation of certain characteristics such as speed and stamina.

Bucking—When a horse flings its hind heels to the sky.

Canter—A three-beat gait which, correctly speaking, is called a collected gallop. A slow gallop or a fast lope.

Champion—The highest award given in a particular division in a horse show. *Reserve Champion* is second to this. The awards are based on the number of points an exhibitor accumulates at a show.

Chip—A momentary hesitation by the horse before jumping a fence.

Class—Specific categories of competition in a horse show, such as Maiden, Local Hunter, Working Hunter, Medal and Maclay.

Counter Canter—A canter on the false, or outside, lead which is maintained by the rider's legs. This movement is designed to improve the horse's balance.

Course—An intricate pattern of numbered fences and directional lines making up the route the horse and rider must take.

Equitation—The art of riding horseback.

Equitation or Horsemanship Classes—The Equitation division is divided into two main classifications—Equitation on the Flat (walk, trot and canter) and Equitation over Jumps. Both are usually limited to children eighteen years old and under. In Equitation jumping classes, the jumps are usually limited to 3 feet 6 inches, and often just 3 feet. Smoothness should characterize jumping and any rough spots should be camouflaged as much as possible.

Exercise Ring—Fenced-in space in which the horse is given a workout or schooling.

First Year Green—A horse show class for hunters. A First Year Green hunter is a horse in his first year of showing in any classes, at a regular AHSA member show requiring horses to jump.

Flying Change of Lead—When a horse changes from one lead to the other at a canter without coming to a trot or reducing his gait. A *simple change* is when the horse is brought down to a walk or trot for not more than four strides, then takes off on the opposite lead.

Fly Sheet—A lightweight mesh blanket used to protect horses from flies.

Gallop—A fast, natural three-beat gait in which the horse moves forward in a leaping and bounding motion. The fastest of the horse's gaits.

Gelding—A neutered stallion.

Grand Prix—A national or international class for jumpers in which large sums of money and expensive goods are awarded as prizes.

Green—An inexperienced horse. One whose schooling is incomplete.

Grooming Kit—Box containing instruments to clean and brush the horse. It usually includes mane and tail comb, scissors, two sponges, hoof pick, hoof oil, body brush and rubber curry comb.

Hand Gallop—An extended canter, not as fast as a full gallop. Because of the action of the horse's hind legs, the rider must get well out of the saddle. This, in turn, encourages the faster pace, since the rider's weight is entirely in her heels, and not on the horse's back.

Hock—The tarsal joint or its region in the hind limb of a horse that corresponds to the ankle in man, but is elevated and bends backward.

Horse Shows—Horse shows are designed mostly to exhibit the skill and/or beauty of the *horse*. Some shows include Equitation classes, too, which judge the rider alone or her riding skills, the clothes she wears, the manner in which she carries herself in the show ring. A *recognized show* is one which is a member of the American Horse Shows Association and is run according to its rules. In addition to recognized shows, there are *local shows*. Though the riders and horses are not the same caliber as those at the big shows, local shows are fun and a stimulus to the beginning rider.

Hunt Cap—Velvet-covered hard hat with cork-lined protective crown, small front visor and a chin strap. In Equitation class, hunt caps must be dark blue, brown or black.

Hunter—Hunter refers to the particular job that is expected of a horse or pony, not his ancestry. A hunter can be a thoroughbred, a quarterhorse or a "cross-breed." This animal should be able to carry his rider across country of various types and gradations of ruggedness comfortably. He should move with long, low effortless strides, conserving his energy. Also, the hunter must be able to jump safely the normal height of fences or obstacles which he finds in his path.

Hunter Over Fences—Class in which each horse is required to jump a series of eight to ten fences. "Fences" used might include a coop, a wall, a gate, brush, or an oxer.

Hunter Seat Equitation—An English-style riding that is used for pleasure riding as well as for showing, hunting and advanced jumping. The rider sits forward in the saddle with knees bent, heels down, ankles flexed in and the calf of the leg touching the horse and slightly behind the girth. The reins are carried in both hands. The rider shortens the stirrups enough so she can rise smoothly off the seat by the simple flexing of her ankles, knees and upper legs.

Jumper—A horse that is judged on his performance over jumps only. Style and manner are not counted. The winner is the horse with the lowest number of faults or penalties. Time is sometimes a factor in choosing the winner. The jumper may be any breed and any conformation.

Junior Hunter—A horse of any age. Junior refers to the rider who is eighteen years old or younger.

Leg Bandages—Bandages which go from the horse's hooves to knees or hocks and are worn for protection when loading and traveling in the van. A bandage is also used on the tail, so it won't get rubbed while traveling.

Limit Class—Class open to horses or riders who have not won six blue ribbons at recognized shows.

Local Hunter—Class for hunters owned by exhibitors who live in the area where the horse show is held.

Longe, or Lunge—A long rein used in schooling, breaking and training the horse. It should be at least 30 feet, be flexible and have a swivelled snap at one end.

Maclay—Hunter-seat horsemanship class sponsored by the ASPCA, the champion being chosen at the National Horse Show. It is the best-known trophy for which juniors can compete each year.

"Made" Horse—An educated equine that is a polished performer.

Maiden—Class open to horses or riders who have not won one blue ribbon at a recognized show in the division in which they are being exhibited.

Medal Class—Competition sponsored by AHSA for horsemanship. The national champion is pinned annually under the auspices of the AHSA at Harrisburg, Pennsylvania.

Novice Class—Class open to horses or riders who have not won three blue ribbons at recognized shows.

Open Class—A class open to horses of any age, size or sex, irrespective of the ribbons won, and in which there is no qualification for the rider.

Open Jumper—A horse considered suitable to compete in the Open class. These horses jump the biggest fences in the jumper division.

Paddock—An enclosed area of grassland used for grazing horses or ponies.

Pinning—The awarding of the ribbons at a horse show.

Point System—For each blue (first) ribbon won at a recognized show, five points on championship are scored; for red (second) three; for yellow (third) two, and for white (fourth) one point. These points count toward year-end high score awards.

Quarterhorse—An alert, muscular breed of horse developed for great endurance.

Saddle Soap—A specially prepared soap applied with a damp sponge for cleaning saddles, bridles and other leather harnesses.

Schooling—The teaching and exercising of horse and rider in the techniques of equitation.

Sitting Trot—Also called jog trot. A rather slow, short striding trot to which the rider would normally sit.

Spooky Horse—An equine that becomes excited or frightened by loud noises or objects such as paper, blowing clothes or flash bulbs.

A Stop—A sudden refusal by a horse in front of a fence. If the horse refuses three times, the horse and rider are eliminated.

Tack—(n) Name given to describe the saddlery used on a horse or pony. (v) To put the horse's tack on him; to saddle and bridle him.

Thoroughbred—An English breed of light, speedy horse used chiefly for racing, and originating from crosses between English mares of uncertain ancestry and Arabian stallions. The thoroughbred is high-spirited, timid and excited to flight.

Trot—A moderately fast gait of a horse in which the legs move in diagonal pairs. It corresponds to human jogging.

Turns on the Forehand—Forehand is the term for the front legs and shoulders of the horse. In turns on the forehand, the horse's haunches move in a circular track around the forehand, which remains close to stationary and acts almost as a pivot. The rider's hands hold the front end in place, and the rider's legs move the hind end around.

Turns on the Haunches—The rider swings the horse's front end around the rear end. The rider's legs hold the rear end in place and his hands move the front end around—or, rather, cue the horse to move it around.

Walk—A four-beat gait of a horse in which the feet strike the ground in the sequence near hind, near fore, off hind, off fore.

Warm-up Class—A preparatory class to acquaint the horses with the course before the main events. Ribbons are awarded, but no points.

Withers—The ridge between the shoulder bones of a horse. It is the highest part of a horse's back behind the neck.

Working Hunter—Any horse that is "hunting sound" and can jump a 3-foot-6 or 4-foot wall safely, in good jumping form. The Local Working Hunter class at horse shows is reserved for hunters that belong to exhibitors who live in the areas where the show is held.